Blue Wine

JOHNS HOPKINS: POETRY AND FICTION
John T. Irwin, general editor

BLUE WINE *and Other Poems*

by John Hollander

THE JOHNS HOPKINS UNIVERSITY PRESS
Baltimore and London

To My Brother

This book has been brought to publication with the
generous assistance of the G. Harry Pouder Fund.

Manufactured in the United States of America

The Johns Hopkins University Press, Baltimore, Maryland 21218
The Johns Hopkins Press Ltd., London

The poems in this volume originally appeared in the
following periodicals, some in slightly different form:
American Scholar: "At the End of the Day"; *Bennington
Review*: "Piano Interlude," "The Game," "The Other Route,"
and "The Old Guitar"; *Canto*: "The Train"; *Georgia Review*:
"August Carving," "Monuments," "Just for the Ride," and "What
Was Happening Later at Night"; *Harper's*: "Another Sky";
Kenyon Review: "Blue Wine"; *New Leader*: "Three of the
Fates"; *The New Yorker*: "Ode to Landscape" and "Nox
Regina," Copyright © 1978 by The New Yorker Magazine, Inc.;
New York Review of Books: "Déjà-Vu," Copyright © 1976 by
the New York Review of Books; *Partisan Review*: "Some of
the Parts," "A Statue of Something," and "The Viewer";
Thames Poetry: "Grass Snake"; *Vanderbilt Poetry
Review*: "What Was Happening Late at Night."

Library of Congress Catalog Number 78-20514

ISBN 0-8018-2209-2 (hardcover)
ISBN 0-8018-2221-1 (paperback)

Library of Congress Cataloging in Publication data
will be found on the last printed page of this book.

Contents

III

(I)

Blue Wine

for Saul Steinberg

1   The winemaker worries over his casks, as the dark juice
    Inside them broods on its own sleep, its ferment of dreaming
    Which will turn out to have been a slow waking after all,
    All that time. This would be true of the red wine or the white;
    But a look inside these barrels of the azure would show
    Nothing. They would be as if filled with what the sky looks like.

2   Three wise old wine people were called in once to consider
    The blueness of the wine. One said: "It is 'actually' not
    Blue; it is a profound red in the cask, but reads as blue
    In the only kind of light that we have to see it by."
    Another said: "The taste is irrelevant—whatever
    Its unique blend of aromas, bouquets, vinosities
    And so forth, the color would make it quite undrinkable."
    A third said nothing: he was lost in a blue study while
    His eyes drank deeply and his wisdom shuddered, that the wine
    Of generality could be so strong and so heady.

3   There are those who will maintain that all this is a matter
    Of water—hopeful water, joyful water got into
    Cool bottles at the right instant of light, the organized
    Reflective blue of its body remembered once the sky
    Was gone, an answer outlasting its forgotten question.
    Or: that the water, colorless at first, collapsed in glass
    Into a blue swoon from which it never need awaken;
    Or: that the water colored in a blush of consciousness
    (Not shame) when it first found that it could see out of itself
    On all sides roundly, save through the dark moon of cork above
    Or through the bottom over which it made its mild surmise.

There are those who maintain this, they who remain happier
With transformations than with immensities like blue wine.

4   He pushed back his chair and squinted through the sunlight
        across
    At the shadowy, distant hills; crickets sang in the sun;
    His mind sang quietly to itself in the breeze, until
    He returned to his cool task of translating the newly
    Discovered fragments of Plutarch's lost essay "On Blue Wine."
    Then the heavy leaves of the rhododendrons scratched against
    Gray shingles outside, not for admittance, but in order
    To echo his pen sighing over filled, quickening leaves.

5   "For External Use Only?" Nothing says exactly that,
    But there are possibilities—a new kind of bluing
    That does not whiten, but intensifies the color of,
    All that it washes. Or used in a puzzle-game: "Is blue
    Wine derived from red or white? emerging from blood-colored
    Dungeons into high freedom? or shivering in the silk
    Robe it wrapped about itself because of a pale yellow chill?"
    One drink of course would put an end to all such questioning.

6   ". . . and when he passed it over to me in the dim firelight,
    I could tell from the feel of the bottle what it was: the
    Marqués de Tontada's own, *El Corazón azul*. I had
    Been given it once in my life before, long ago, and
    I tell you, Dan, I will never forget the moment when
    It became clear, before those embers, that the famous blue
    Color of the stuff could come to mean so little, could change
    The contingent hue of its significance: the truer
    To its blue the wine remained, the less it seemed to matter.
    I think, Dan, that was what we had been made to learn that night."

7   This happened once: Our master, weary of our quarreling,
    Laughed at the barrel, then motioned toward us for a drink; and
    Lo, out of the sullen wooden spigot came the blue wine!

4

8 And all that long morning the fair wind that had carried them
  From isle to isle—past the gnashing rocks to leeward and around
  The dark vortex that had been known to display in its whorls
  Parts not of ships nor men but of what it could never have
  Swallowed down from above—the fair wind blew them closer to
  The last island of all, upon the westernmost side of
  Which high cliffs led up to a great place of shining columns
  That reddened in the sunset when clouds gathered there. They
    sailed
  Neither toward this nor toward the eastern cape, darkened by low
  Rocks marching out from the land in raging battle with the
  Water; they sailed around a point extending toward them,
    through
  A narrow bay, and landed at a very ancient place.
  Here widely-scattered low trees were watching them from the
    hills.
  In huge casks half-buried there lay aging the wine of the
  Island and, weary half to madness, they paused there to drink.
  This was the spot where, ages before even their time, Bhel
  Blazed out in all his various radiances, before
  The jealousy of Kel led to his being smashed, as all
  The old tales tell, and to the hiding and the parceling
  Out of all the pieces of Bhel's shining. Brightness of flame,
  Of blinding bleakness, of flavescent gold, of deepening
  Blush-color, of the shining black of obsidian that
  Is all of surface, all a memory of unified
  Light—all these were seeded far about. There only remained
  The constant fraction, which, even after every sky
  Had been drenched in its color, never wandered from this spot.
  And thus it was: they poured the slow wine out unmingled with
  Water and saw, startled, sloshing up against the insides
  Of their gold cups, sparkling, almost salty, the sea-bright wine . . .

9 It would soon be sundown and a shawl of purple shadow
  Fell over the muttering shoulders of the old land, fair

5

Hills and foul dales alike, singing of noon grass or Spanish
Matters. The wooden farmhouses grew grayer and the one
We finally stopped at, darker than the others, opened its
Shutters and the light inside poured over the patio.
Voices and chairs clattered: we were welcomed and the youngest
Child came forth holding with both hands a jug of the local wine.
It was blue: reality is so Californian.

10   Under the Old Law it was seldom permitted to drink
Blue wine, and then only on the Eight Firmamental
Days; and we who no longer kept commandments of that sort
Still liked to remember that for so long it mattered so
Much that they were kept. And thus the domestic reticence
In my family about breaking it out too often:
We waited for when there was an embargo on the red,
Say, or when the white had failed because of undue rain.
Then Father would come up from the cellar with an abashed
Smile, in itself a kind of label for the dark bottle.
At four years old I hid my gaze one night when it was poured.

11   Perhaps this is all some kind of figure—the thing contained
For the container—and it is these green bottles themselves,
Resembling ordinary one, that are remarkable
In that their shapes create the new wines—*Das Rheinblau,
    Château
La Tour d'Eau, Romanée Cerulée*, even the funny old
Half-forgotten *Vin Albastru*. And the common inks of
Day and night that we color the water with a drop of
Or use for parodies of the famous labels: these as
Well become part of the figuring by which one has put
Blue wine in bold bottles and lined them up against the light
There in a window. When some unexpected visitor
Drops in and sees these bottles of blue wine, and does not ask
At the time what they mean, he may take some drops home with
    him
In the clear cup of his own eye, to see what he will see.

August Carving

Your file which whispers against the piece of silent limestone,
Urging a pair of joined figures into the life of light,
Is echoing the crickets working away at the air
This side of the far cornfield. The cornfield itself mirrors
Something very distant, some place of green, some steadfastness.
The figures coming into stone being commemorate
Our consciousness of bodies' joining, a knowledge as of
Distant light composed here by the green of fields, distant stone
Echoed in these gray blocks resting in the afternoon grass.
The stone pair have been making love but that is as nothing:
The he and she celebrate the embrace of light and stone.
Light will fall from them, as from ourselves: they will pass among
Moments of astonishing shadow, then enter the dark,
Coldly, invisibly, forms fractured from their radiance.

Some of the Parts

In the assurance of oncoming twilight that there is
A vast, pliable space containing regions of our life
That keep entirely in touch, day and night will not crack
Apart. The light on the cold grass will leave slowly, rising
Out of sight, and its claim on colors will be relinquished.
All surfaces will tacitly assent to this. The shell
Of night will start singing into the ear of the day's shell,
And they will have been washed in the one sea that is all depth
And no surface, yea, even like the little pond dwelling
Off in the near corner of the audible world, waveless,
Bottomless, but brimming with an encouraging chorus
Of sounding night. Remembering which, in the swarm of noon's
Tiny-winged exigencies, will flake apart the promise
Of it, lying in the sun like the pieces of some dream.

Monuments

for Natalie Charkow

Start here: something has exhaled this marble and moved
On, itself a kind of wind. Yet what blows among
The carvings now and the polished tablets can feel
Nothing of the stone it touches, which feels nothing
Of air. And could it grab your hand and lead you toward
A momentary splendor—against the sky soaked
In blue a Great Spangled Fritillary hanging
Among the white tombs—this would have been a picture
Only of the remembrance of connection,
A quick fable of fragile wings alighting on
Heavy slabs sunk in the darkness of earth, telling
No tall truth, flourishing in no parable field.

No more to worry then at the dry leaf blowing
Against whatever text has been cut into stone.
A plaything of the daughters of marble and the
Descendants of wind, it should urge no eye to rest
In mid-journey upon its marginalia.
For in the conditional truth of turf, here lies
Stone, whose inscriptions keep being sure of what was
Not, by way of hedging about what was: bodies
Now grounded below pain who lay above in life
Sleeping in beds of white, dreaming the blank, black ground.
Bodies who, when pain came in such a sleep, would grow
A limb of hurt to be the place where pain would lie.

And what members of joy grew up at the sweet touch
Of heart laying sure hands on body from within
Are pictured only now in shapes under the grass,

Always dreaming these headstones, steles, chiseled urns,
Wreaths and leaves in low relief of sleep: Oh see,
Here is a red mirror of shining porphyry
In whose glow the eye observes itself observing
Itself, and on and on like that. Here is repose,
Figured in the stone pair lying above the ground,
Her knees raised and touching, he on his side by hers.
And here, worn down by the rages of wind and rain,
Two shapeless doggies keep faith with a broken slab.

And then, blocking the way of going on among
The memorials, seeming to face us from all
Corners from wherever we come toward it, that Face
Dangles from its snaky hairdo, cold, half-smiling
So that even close up its mouth waits in the near
Distance. No old, contorted visage of horror
We know from wisdom's shield regards us in this clear,
Gray afternoon light that calls the craziest greens
Forth from themselves. It is another gaze, as from
Memorials of our own we once made, that now
Would petrify our eyes and turn our tongues to grass.
It is as if we made her in our images.

So that, fleeing back down the cold, light, roofless aisles
Where recall bounces back from unechoing stones,
We rerun mazes of our late meandering
Among these short, arresting inscriptions and this
Smarmy memorializing. We bump against
Knowing that it was not in pursuit of solid
Pictures that we wandered in among all this, but
That there need be no seeking that which sleeps away
In stone for which the living butterfly is but
An image, as of its own fluttering shadow;
That the tombstones were there wherever we were then,
Where we are now, wherever there is wandering.

Thus what we should have wanted all along—boxes
Of glass, showing through it the grass, other boxes,
And some of the sky from which the eye turns, flying
Its own unlikeness—now seem a last resort, not
To be found anymore. And here where space seems now
To be carved out of the bright stone that shadows it,
Perhaps a monument of eternal crystal
Might yet remain one with what it recollected,
And with reflections on and in it. It would be
More difficult to enter than one of those stone
Closed doorways cut into the sky, the grass. It would
Be empty of itself, and bright with what was meant.

A Statue of Something

The great wooden figure of The River is finished, and yellow
And brown shadows attach themselves to the interior
Of the sculptor's studio, where he stands holding the hand
Of the short, naked lady as she steps down from her platform.
He is leading his model out into interpretation,
Life after art, re-engagement with a world whose shadows
Are insubstantial and always full of motion.
They are like the surface of water on the river
In which the model will swim, rejoining a broken
Circle of representations dancing in the sunlight,
Given a common substance by their chorus of shadows:
Presiding wood, fresh water, unpainted flesh,
On which the inland waves flash with an excitement
Beyond mere grandeur, more fragile than the language of shadow
With which, for example, a painter might make his own
Late afternoon representations to the spirit of figures,
Showing all this, what it had been about.

Ode to Landscape

"O, beautiful for specious skies," you
Sang, as if to laugh off what is so
   Serious about space
   Of this kind: that in it

There occur evidences which clouds
Come to witness, gathering with more
   Than curiosity
   To read their own shadows

Mottling tawny acres of stubble
With purpling tones, but staying to see
   More than they had crowded
   Into a picture for

—The whole reasonable world, the wide
Kingdom of all middle distances.
   The Dutch who depicted
   Their dinners against a

Sacramental black background had sky
Enough to give away; but their gray,
   Hopeful clouds seemed to catch
   Doubt from the ground's places

Where nothing much happens but shadows.
But that is right, in a world whose heights
   Are joined to their baseness
   Like sky glued to the ground

Here in this picture, or that picture.
The matter of the starry skies and
    The great Word they entail
    As eyes lower in praise

Toward textual ground, or turn inward,
Is not at issue in painted clouds.
    No: the lesson learned is
    An introduction to

Radiance, the early paradigms
Of the distinct, whether brushed up from
    Surroundings, or ruled by
    Stern lines, no matter how

Bending. And, the lesson learned, we move
Beyond the picture plain to fancy
    Spaces and colors that
    Inhere in things, not light

Nor pigment nor other colored things—
All the messiness of what is there—
    Bearing with us a gift
    Of brightness understood

Not for us, but for nature, given
In return for contingent likeness
    Being taken from her
    By *Pastoral Landscape*

Etcetera, with which I shall come
Down to your raw countryside of corn
    And stone barns to see you,
    I think, in a few days.

Three of the Fates

CLOTHO

The spinster: it would be given to no
Mother to make this thread of short fibers
That twistingly stretch into years—that would
Be too true. And suppose these three sisters
Were all crammed into one mother who did
The three things? All we could do is regard
That huge fable, know its truth, and vomit.
She brings us into the world only with
Her hands, no longer a mere girl at her
Spinning; and what she may remember or
Have ever known of love puzzles us—we
Can never hear her humming some old tune,
Older than winds; we are not allowed to
Suppose that she is some poor semi-comic
Dummy like ourselves, hopefully spinning
A rope of escape for some loved one, duped
By her sisters, or by someone beyond.
No: the thread that seems unending, and
That seems unendingly to be being
Spun, is made only that it can be cut.
Among her and her sisters a dark sort
Of motherhood is there all right, but still
The old tale will only tell of coldness
And utter distance among the high crags.

LACHESIS

Random measurer: why is it that all
We can do in her case is to question?
Asking if some pretty code of roughness
In the wrapped strands of fiber leads her to
Declare that some length is now at an end,
Asking whether she sits and deciphers
Such messages—is this not all our play?
Asking what we are to do when our play,
As with this very figure, fancying
Up the old fiction for a moment, ends—
Is this not all our late work? O, what book
Of random digits does she use? What way
Of casting lots, what chance does she choose? As
If in answer, the sharp winds of whether
It matters or not alternately rise
And fall in no necessary order.

ATROPOS

A trope? There are no tropes where the thread is
Cut there is no turning of strands, no twist
Of the literal line of cord. And then
Even the literal unravels: that
Is when we most need the intertwining,
The turning, the making taught, in order
That the rope lie right. But neither the pure
Straight nor the twisted straight are there any
More: here are only frayed fibers, as if
Gone back to an original dead grass.

Grass Snake

Had there been no green in him one would not have thought
Him to have been envenomed, but starting back from the
Darting of this virid twister, one forgets at least
For a moment that there is no question of his virulence here.
His color is drawn from the grass in which he flickers,
But washed as by the water colorist's hand that had
Drawn the whole snake from nature. And it is for that—
For the garment of the benign he wears—that we recoil
From his intrusions as we do not from those of most
Of his brothers, black, striped or evilly mottled.
In junkyards, motionless lengths of rotten tubing.
Or rusted coils of spring; on battered, gray sidewalks,
The half-dried, gray serpent-stump an unleashed dog left
To affront the carelessness of our steps; and in the Garden
Of Parodies, some creature like the ambiguous Slank—all these
Subtle questioners of our state are of the same tribe
As the green one, one with the ambiance through which they creep,
Presence unwrenched from a background, startling, until rescued
By what we know of the world, to our alien eyesight.

The Train

The dreamers lie like sections
Of curved track from a toy train
That will not make a neat concentric fit (the
Inner radius of curvature of each
Not being equal to that of the outer)
And if not like dreaming rails abuzz with one
Another's trembling, and if
Unconformingly in touch, then yet bedded
By their ties in a road of
Some soft sort. Outside, clattered
Freight of daylight goes by half heard only; their
Hearing cannot count out the
Innocent childhood rhymes of
Passing: *cattlecar, coalcar, boxcar, flatcar*
(Caboose! sneezing by at the
End of sound as the obscured
Quiet hillside becomes plain again). They have
Uncoupled, the dreamers, after the throbbing
Train, long halted in the soft
Tunnel, has backed out into daylight again.

Was it that the train had lain
Safe in the tunnel, that the hole in the long
Hill was home? It awoke there
To a lowered roar after a flashing by
Of wan marsh grasses, cattails
Brushing up grays in the miserable air:
After these flashing by past
Glass there came the running by
Of the small walls of darkness.
The stiff train lay in its strait

Funnel at the time that the
Sleepers began their nocturnal journeyings.

Sleepers lie under the rails.
They travel backward, the hard crossties that could
Crack hatchets, lying under the singing track.
The rails dream of rhyming; they
Turn into verse, endless lines
Not measured in sevens or in elevens,
Say, but continuing on
Into a converging strip.
They dream the epic of gleaming and distant
Vanishing, and diminution of time, and
They sleep dreamlessly under phrases of roar
And passages of clicking
Wheels. And these soft rails, the two
Dreamers, are being children of eleven,
Say, and of seven, and their funny dreams are
Of boxcars loaded with chattering white dice
(Seven meanwhile awakens,
Trembling, in the matter of a skull, or so
The shorter dreamer remembers). Remember
That they are poised yet in their
Sojourn of waking: they do
Not dream of these dreams. But as
The pliant engine gathers its wits back from
A sweet dream deep in the tunnel in the hill
As if drawn by its tender
Out of the inner lamplit red into blue
Light of outer night, one recalled an old dream:

Which same came running: the great
High track of night, the elevated structure
Of blackened steel higher than

High, swerving across most of the horizon,
Curving into a station
Perched like a box atop it.
The most important train ran
Along there carrying one
Across the unfamiliar
Fields of a city that was
At once one's own and unknown.
The tracks were too high. At the
End of the journey everything was too low:
One was underground more deeply than one had
Been above it, in vast caverns of brown hewn
Stone, Piranesian vaults, complex levels
Of track and tunnel opening into the
Deepest hall of all. The train
That had run on rails too tall
Now paused by a wall too low—as if a clock
One needed to live by was always missing
The satisfying cardinal verticals
And could only read seven
Or eleven o'clock, too soon or too late.
This was the dark place of loss.

The other recalled her own
Way, not of rail but concrete:
Unplucked cloverleaves lying
Among each other, woven
Into a frightful chain from
Which there was no escaping—
A frightening on highways
From which there was no turning
Off, ways neither through the dark
Nor free of it whirled around
The looping of things, and back.

Then the tenderly retired engine, the
Emptied tunnel softly regathering its
Inner darknesses, were silent; the roaring
One made in the other slept.
The dreamers felt no sound, and heard nothing of
The moist music of places where the landscape
Was shaded by their touching: soft bush against
Curving track of rump, tributary fingers
Lost among meadows of tresses, all silent;
While flying high overhead in the sunlit blue
A tiny unheard train inches along the
Frail trestle of wisdom, seemingly never
To complete the long crossing.
They are and they were: here, there;
The one, the other; the train,
The tunnel. And just as there
Had been within here, and then
Had driven deep into now,
And as the engine had made
A haven in the hill, so the dream of one
Drew up into the tunnel of the other's,
And waits there now at the Station of Loss,
Being the dream of the last departing train.

This roadbed is at the right
Height: here is none of his high
Impossible trestle or
His dungeon terminal. Nor
Is she here in her poor car
Missing the points of turning
Off: it is to his dreaming
Eye, not hers, that the last trace
Of fear adheres—a travel
Poster on a far platform

Wall shows on a green ground a
White unlucky cloverleaf
Leading screamingly along
Into itself; but this was
Never his fear. Here in their
Interpenetrating dreams
The awaited train arrives
Jerkily. They are to board.
But it starts again. And stops.
He runs a few yards farther
Down the platform. Then it stops.
Then it starts again. By now
He can see her standing with
Two small personages far
Back along the platform, bathed
In a light of waiting, and
He knows that no matter what
Happens in the matter of
The train they will wait for him.
She sees the train come and go.
Then the train starts up again.
Rushing toward it, she perceives
The conductor leaning out
A passing window—his mouth
Looks grievously like wet meat.
That is why the train cannot
Wait and why it cannot stop.
She awakens, having missed
The same train. She is in him.

He wakens. They recall
White, high ways, soft, tubular
Buildings, mauve and lemon, tiny ovoid cars
Sliding along the roads and sighing around

The cloverleaf model in handsome plaster,
While the slow train of benches giving on
This visionary scene of what the City
To Come—perhaps West Alabaster—would be,
Snaked through the tunnel of the Fair and floated
Redundant through the mazes of dream undimmed.
He and she sat there a year apart and
Emerged into sunlight wearing a button
Saying *I Have Seen the Future*. They had not.

Neither have they heard the past, wherein huge, black
Engines released steam and shiny pistons danced
Steel sarabands: neither has the sound of the
Last fast train awakened them;

Passing beyond their window into darkness,
The train runs through them as they each withdraw now
From the unending tunnel of the other.
They turn over once and lie,

Cast there like unwise dice, their numbers covered
(Seven? Eleven?) by the bedclothes, their sleep,
Emptied of dream, resembling more and more its
Ultimate older brother,

And not those twin cousins of slumber, tunnel
And train, receding in the rising morning
Light, the tunnel's mouth overgrown, the engine
Shriveled, the paired rails twisted,

The roadbed rumpled, the clear and distinct cars
Dulled in a painterly blue, the sleepers ripped
Up by the tumult of the earth and lying
Merely among each other,

Like the awakened dreamers, who rise now in
The rinsed sight of each other, entrained bravely
For the day, for the long ailing day, seven
Until eleven, and then

Trailing off into far distance, the train of
Thought awaits their lying down in the Stations
Of Sleep; they will count slowly passing cars and
Board one, a dark one, at last.

(II)

LYRICAL INTERVAL

Song-Cycle for Piano and Low Voice

Prologue

AM KLAVIER (at the Piano)

The evening light dies down: all the old songs begin
To crowd the soft air, choiring confusedly.
Then above that sea of immense complexities
The clear tenor of memory I did not know
I had enters; like a rod of text held out by
A god of meaning, it governs the high, wayward
Waves of what is always going on in the world.
All that becomes accompaniment. And it is
What we start out with now: this is no time
To pluck or harp on antiquities of feeling.
These soft hammers give gentle blows to all their strings,
Blows that strike with a touch of challenge and of love.
Thus what we are, being sung against what we come
To be a part of, rises like a kind of light.

First Echo

Their answer was here before my
    Question touched this place;
These echoes were recorded here
    In another time:
The brook rumored of Sicily;
    The trees' whispering
Was of the Arcadian pines,
    And once wooden flutes
Inscribed sound in the hollows of
    These loud-speaking stones.
And there the joyful, distant yell
    Of a climber died
In wreaths of echo on the hill.
    All these voices still
Echo my outcry of your name.
    Is it truth they tell?
Or are they truthful to this place,
    Merely, and very old?

The Cable-Car

The cable-car is the easy way up
The great mountain we see from everywhere
And whose shadow falls outside the city.

The cable-car is the easy way up,
And as it swings on above dark ravines
I catch the first sight of her distant home.

The cable-car is the easy way up,
And thus I am breathless here at the top
Not from climbing, but at how far I see.

How high it is here, and how far I see!
From her window she cannot see how near
Her house is to the highway into town.

How high it is here, and how far I see!
The world we both move in is its own map:
From here, my house looks very near to hers.

How far it is here to the ground again!
I shall descend with joy, as if rising.
The cable-car is the long, slow way down.

Eyes

Dark lamps whose fire is all their own,
But whose light may be coming from
The candle here on the table.
I search them and I say nothing.

As I touch your hand my fingers
Are more certain of what they know
Than my own caressing eyes are.
What they know—how much is that worth?

Calling across Water

The dark pines are silent now, and the thrush
    Amid them is hushed.
Water laps at the shore of my island.
    It is all silence
In the middle of the lake between us,
    You there and I here.
The lapping is the nonsense of nature,
    But the wide water
Bears the clear sound of my call across it.
    It is not longing,
It is all the wideness of dark water,
    It is our quiet
Enislement which makes of this dimmed, distant
    Speech a mode of song.

The Patch of Garden

Two round, lovely hills stand above
The long descent of fair meadow
Down to where the small garden lies.
Shall we be there, as if once more
In the true place we were before?

The dry angel of day has turned
Away for a moment: leave him
To guard ruined temples among
The stony fields and the dead hills.

Quickly now, he is not looking:
Let us enter your own garden
Through the gateway in the soft hedge.
We shall be there, as if once more
In the true place we were before.

Land and Water

We rode gently over evening fields
Together: we were our own one steed.
　　Faster and faster we went
Until no trees swept by: they became
Part of the color of ground and sky.
　　And when the great hedge loomed up
Then we took it in a long, slow leap.
　　Now in our dark, soundless boat
　　We lie on the wide water.

Piano Interlude

The air is emptied of song in this gentleness;
Our bed is by the window, and our own silence
Is like a curtain drawn back, allowing moonlight
To come harping through the window-blinds. Silver strings
Quiver on the ceiling, and here your heartbeat half-
Enters my ear; my text is your skin on my tongue;
Below us our limbs are composed in a tender
And intricate figure not to be read aloud.
Song is not born in rooms emptied by fulfillment,
But only in long, cold halls, hollow with desire.

The Game

What if you were to disappear?
Should I then run to the police?
Would I wave at them a list of
Everything I loved in you? Would
I sing out a full description,
Every adjective a kind of
Kiss? Would I have spirited you
Away somewhere myself so that
I should have a chance to say what
You were, and how you were lovely?
Would you have hidden yourself
In order to hear it? Venus
Once mislaid her boy and blazoned
His description to the waiting
World: nobody who has told that
Tale thinks it was an accident.

The Movie

The old picture plays
Lights across the screen.
Overhead, the beam
From the thoughtful booth
Flickers in a kind
Of code that only
The screen can read out.

Lights like memories
Flicker on the screen
Of your deep gazing.
My eyes and my hand
Are like some part of
The surrounding dark.

The Dying Friend

I visited him at noon.
Even so, he lay in a
Kind of darkening; the light
From outside intruded there,
Part of some other picture.
I missed you there, then and now.

Then I came back here, hoping
To find you, with drawn shades in
Bed, to kindle what we could
Of dark warmth, while outside lay
A cold, continuing light.
I missed you there, then and now.

The Dream

I run down the streets
Of dim houses, low,
Narrow and of few
Windows, looking down
Corners to find her.

There she stands under
An unlit streetlamp,
Smiling with someone
Else over what had
Been our own old joke.

Then I wake, moaning.
Why, O why? All this
Need not have been a dream:
It is what I see
With my opened eye.

Why does sleep reveal
What the day has not
Hidden, as if it
Were a dark secret
My heart could not keep?

Lying Down

He who is upright when he lies beside you,
Rhyming breath with breath,
Curve with curve,
Plays you false: his force with a little mind of
Its own, reaches toward
You, below,
And as, above, he looks into your eyes, lies.

The Other Route

Yours is the way I no longer take.
Familiar streets, corners I passed by,
Corners I turned—all these old neighbors
Will soon be ordinarily strange.

Along the wet walls outside bare trees
I wait and decide not to walk now
In the cold park, but that ghost of me
Who would have gone your way enters there.

He then, not I, ambles by the lake
Distractedly, he who is robbed there,
And stabbed in the empty summer-house,
And who lies dead then in the damp leaves.

His way is gone. He has gone away.
But there are more ghosts. I cannot kill
Them off so readily. The dim streets
Begin to be crowded with shadows.

The Park

Here on these benches in the wan sun
Ancient couples sit and wait for death.
They absorb what they can of the wide
Field of uncaring life around them.
I shall never have grown into old
Winter with you now: has time robbed me
Of waiting with you here, or spared me?

Last Echo

Echo has the last word,
But she loses the rest,
Giving in to silence
After too little time.
And, after all, what is
A last word, then? After
All the truth has been told—
No more than a cold rhyme.

The Old Guitar

I take down the old guitar from the wall,
Instrument of the idle, and silent—
What can it say for me? I only hear
An ailing wind blow through my dead fingers.

I feel only the chill of silence there.
And just as well—suppose I plucked the fruit
Of trellised chords: how would this hollow shell
Shaped like an absent body, then resound?

Wildly, like the roaring wind's melody,
Only an echo of its malady.
Like the blackened waters of a midnight
River running deep inside a closed book.

(III)

Just for the Ride

for John Ashbery

I shall get on
This bus with its destination
Rolled up out of sight like an eye
Showing only
A blank grey strip to tell me where
It is going:
The bus seems to be stopping at
Every fourth or eighth corner.

It is as if the traffic lights
Were going red and green by some
System of brakes the bus itself
Put on all possible motion.

Aside from this
I noticed nothing within it
Any more remarkable than
What is outside it, such as how
Momentary mouthfuls of steam
Scud across the watertanks up
There looking like something wrong with
A way of seeing watertanks.

Now it has stopped.
Now, getting on
With it, it sighs
With released steam.

Down the cheapening streets it goes
In search of an exegete of
Blank, grey strips, the
Falling sleet along the windows
Pasting invisibilities
Over the glass mind of the bus,
Layering its falseface eyes with
Ice in light strips.

Behind those grey
Unlit headlights,
Eyeglasses for
Glass eyes, no motor reposes;
Only the driver peering through
Strips in the grey windshield: why did
There not appear
To be sleet falling earlier?

Has the bus got
Drunk on its ride?
Its uncertain
Course through districts
Unconnected by bus to each
Other runs downhill now until
Just before a
Pause, I look up from a low point:

Far on the road ahead, at a
Hilltop, two distant buses one
Coming, one going go by: for
A moment they kiss in passing.

In pausing the bus switches off
The backward travels of storefronts
And old cars parked

On downhill slopes.
Now inside it there is motion,
If only of noticing: the
Interior travelers glance
Up at the few advertisements
In between blue
Gaps overhead.
They read of relief from pain and
Love and spruce-screened
Middle distances and beauty
Preparations and openings
For young women.
Then the pause stops and the bus starts.

And if with a
Jerk, at least so
As to move upward along the
Long slope ahead
As if that matter—of going
On up—were what was happening
Inside the bus, and not merely
Recorded there by the glances
Turned back toward the special section
Reserved for those mutilated
In the war: the slow crawl of the
Telephone poles
Down toward one,
The near-motionlessness of a
Very distant house across some
Meaningless fields,
The sense of the
Center strip being gobbled up
In perspective by the bus's
Left front corner,
The dark green mob

Of foliage kept from the right
Of the road by a strip of sand—
These occur internally too.

So that the violence of light
Raking through the hot windows as
The bus creeps out
From a long underpass is no
Noble action,
Nor is its derived fiction in
The echoing reflection of
Galloping shadows on the plain
Faces a major chronicle.
It is as if those faces were
Glass behind which
All unreflected light intrudes.

Not that there is any lack of
Incident on buses—a man
Stretched out on the back seat may be
Dead; the sombre people halfway
Forward may indeed be doing
Each other with crossed hands under
The spread-out raincoat; just beyond
The flat joke of Kenneth, Kansas,
On some night-riding long-distance
Bus a baby might be being
Delivered in a guitar-case:
These would not happen to the bus.

These would happen
In the part of the world the bus
Happened to be swallowing up
At the moment,
Even the part

This urban bus on the wrong route,
Almost lost in this bare country,
Slowly devours,
As in seeming
Morning now it cuts the roadside
Small grass with its scythe of shadow,
Thin and narrowed,
Leaving unmown
The promising corn beyond, the
Road of return on the near left.
This bus, though, was
Surely never
Intended to return that way.
Or even by a wider loop—
Some ox-bow of
Road wandering
Around hills and under bridges
Until, weary in the reddened
Afternoon sun,
A bus crawling
Up a hill would pass so close to
Its outward road that a rider
Would wonder why
The roadway was
Duplicated by another
Parallel one, running by so
Near to his own.

But as often at the end of
Journeyings when the unchosen
Alternatives seem more vivid
Than the way taken—when what was
Rejected for not being quite
The way of putting it; jostling
In the consciousness, armed with their

Late clarity, here where the bus
Is soon to end its branchless route,
All the possible turnings it
Never made edge the rows of seats,
As shadows of the unexamined
Parts of the day edge a lawn at
Sundown, dark borders becoming
A shore by the widening green.
Now, a last stop.

From it I can only walk away in wonder
At how close to home I believe myself to be,
With no grounds for assuming that I am even
In the neighborhood of where I boarded the bus
And not at the other end of the wide town, where
Night has risen from the vacant sidewalks like dew
Seemingly wept up by darkened grass: perhaps one
Felt a right to have returned, without contrivance,
One felt motion forward to bear a promise of
Periphery. Now only a short walk, or what
Will turn out to be too long, will tell; behind me
The bus has turned on ever-burning border lights.

What Was Happening Late at Night

He was searching all the pages by lamplight for himself
But there was no speculum in the soft text, giving him
His difficult, raw images. The pages held pictures of
Desire for error mirrored in the errors of desire.
Hard surfaces that give most of the light and take of none
Are far less generous than the dark, in which we perceive
What we are now verily, what all shall come to for us.

The roses of music had blown and blasted; from the cool
Unwithering summer dark, echoes of silences dressed
Into neat blocks sailed through air, the window near his chair, then
Entered his ear and built there walls of deafness surrounding
The empty city he would become, walls of dead echo,
The fingers of the wind slept across the pines; only from
The book's pale chords wild powers in the lamplight plucked a song.

What Was Happening
Later at Night

He had counted the dropping stars on flagrant nights, and stood
Waiting for one to fall along the fell plumbline his eye
Had dropped, through the dark of nothingness that lay all below
The palpable black waiting unreachably beyond that.
But what he looked out at were the rebel angles the stars
Took in their occasional flashes, the oblique, unaimed
Whizzings of the Olympian squibs, fallen to nothing.
This was the vast, general accident still going on.
And yet it needed his grounded eye to mark the dropping;
To water with searing tears (not his) dark fields of utmost
Gravity; to ogle the acute scintillations of
All the countless seen and unseen others, too grand to act.
There they were: his head reeled, the plumbline swerved in the
     darkness
As if his small falling eye could have brought all down with it.

Another Sky

The Thing in the mirror neither greeted me nor reproached,
And yet I would avoid it, not so much for its power
To make me mime its inflections of visage—a set of
The mouth, a tangle of doubt under the brow—as for the
Flattening of self—the reduction of within to behind,
The loss of voice to a wind blown at bright glass. I would turn
Away from it, lest I become a movement of shadow
Across a surface too. The more I denied it my light
The more it starved, the while I fed on what reflected me
In the round light in the clear flesh of your returning gaze.
Now there is no truth in the vacated spaces. Your eyes
Turned away: I must see myself in my own, the eyes kept
Under silvery wraps which must never be shattered, and
In whose gray pools, lit with rainy light, I must never drown.

The New Notebook

These faintly reassuring lines,
Gray and reasonably spaced in a field of fainter gray
We may as well call white—

Are they the traces of tradition?
Are they in themselves the tradition being nearly at one
With the words that walk them?

Or do our forebears silently inhere
In the very characters we feel to be so fresh
(Shaken from morning leaves

Or struck from the dry night rock
Or shaken like tears of joy from a dancer on the hill)
Falling into their places

In the newly blued space
Between those lines merely unused yet and unable
Themselves to rule?

We shall see where we make them
Take us, as guides or as the faint shadows by whom we walk
Hand in hand with ourselves.

The Notebook Labeled "Jealousy"

Jealousy: hidden in the shallow worldliness of a French moral vocabulary, the simple Greek for "zeal."

Jealousy bored a hole in the garden wall and saw thornbushes, as he had hoped, but blighted with occasional roses. For his pains, a vision of pain.

Later, he crawled before her feet, his knees and nose to the ground. After a few years of this, he came to believe himself to be in diligent search of fallen coins.

A man husbands his secret for the same reason that he loves cities. In a world of contingent openness—framed skies; estuaries shackled by bridges; stunted and dusty sycamores, peeling in smoky air—it is the deepest closures that bring the heart to leaping: peeping out of a glass cell into fields of fallen starlight; facing down carpeted corridors that pause, softly lit, in the moment of hope, rather than echoing stonily with the footsteps of memory; lying in love's warm tunnel, concentric in cunt, in body, in bed, in room, in flat, in stony space, in night, in hiding. The hole is the first circle. It knows the last secret.

Jealousy behind his blind; the slats are just right; he is sliced by their shadows. "The real world is merely the shadow of that assurance of eventual experience which accompanies sanity" (Santayana): Jealousy behind his blind misunderstands this.

Jealousy on a summer night: His strings are untuned; music dies about him in the warm air. Then, from the terrace by the lake, a chord of the diminished seventh rises up to the lawn. He looks— there is nothing but a chain of lights across the dark water. But inner strings vibrate sympathetically; they had, in fact, been tuned for just this moment—his knee trembles like the agitated string of a cello as he sits in a wicker chair, amid confused sounds of crickets from the grass rising like a roar of dark green blood. Motionless, he is already in quest of a peculiar melody.

Desire longs for original possession, for a walk along the warm causeway, for a first look at the morning hills, for an initial plunge into the quickening cave. Jealousy lusts *after* them, as we say, fearing what he most desires, to be pitied.

Envious of his sons who outlive him;
Unwilling to initiate because it prevents concluding;
Unwilling to be Alpha because that is not to be Omega
And to be last is to be first—
"Where does it end?" asks Jealousy, burning with hope that it does not.

The Viewer

for M.

In the room of your dream even
A senseless instrument like this
Seemed wholly natural: lenses,
Neat body, and squared-off sets of
Hairlines for framing a round world
Within right angles. The problem
When you awoke was not the room
Of joy you had been in but what
Was given you there to perceive
It with—and what to do with it.
First, it mattered that it took no
Photos, like the dream itself, had
Needs be used only then and there.
It was no mirroring globe which
Seemed a world of glass, like the round
Mirror Britomart found waiting
In her father's closet. It was
No teloptic picture like the
One from which Pamina peered out
At her seer. It was no window
Into a small, bright room in which
A passerby might see held in
The momentary mullions of
Its frame young Van Dyck promising
Nothing in particular save
That his image would not fade with
Oncoming of awakening.
(Though silvering behind the world's
Glass had faded in a time of

Brightening light: that glass became
Transparent and long since has lost
Its ability to reflect.)
In our time we have come to see
Through the glass, to want to enter
The bright ball whose bottom is deep
In its center.—So that even
To have carried back the viewer
Intact from the lovely chamber
Of your sleep like some insistent
Rare seashell, is to be left quite
Stranded on this shore of meanings
Where the uses of things harden
Underfoot even as we walk
Slowly up the refusing dunes.
It would reduce your yellow room
To its own neat scale; it could not
Take a picture but at best could
Borrow one. The viewer you need
Would have to show what you cannot
See without it, the transparent
Fiction purely dwelling among
All the furnishings of space. So
That one only need report what
The viewer showed; one's disclosures
Would have the glassiness of clear
Inventory; they would need no
Busy surfaces, worked up with
Splendid energies; they would need
No urgent frame. They would live in
Reviewing their originals.
Thus if your dreams one week were all
Of water, lost in the sieve of
Waking, no way of perceiving
Would vanish in mist; there would be

Transparency still, through, and of
Which there would be the light, the light
Of what is to be seen, sounding
Through the clear bell of where you are.

Déjà-Vu

It is as if they were part of this struggle for transparency
That goes on and on—I mean those moments that transports
Of remembering choose for their flabbergasting act:
The casual meal in the normal course of ordinaries
At which Brenda asks for the ketchup, for instance, just after,
So it seems, we remembered that she would. And suppose
That she had behaved extraordinarily and said
"Pass the Kappock," or that a newt had occurred in the pitcher
Of milk: there would have been nothing alarming about it.
It would merely have been surprising; whatever grips our
Minds at those moments of "Here it is" would be eased
By astonishment; and afterwards as we total up
These common instants inexplicably crowned with fearfulness,
It is like turning leaves in an old novel, wondering
Why the engravings of the most uninteresting and unpicturesque
Scenes should have been the ones to be so wildly hand-colored.
But that is as it should be—no deep magic of unknowing,
None of the mind's secret raids on its own storehouses,
Occasions these images of reminding. It is probably
Only a matter of circuitry, of the alpha-rhythm's
Interruption, that makes the here and now enter
The known by the back gate used for returning visitors,
And all with the irrelevance of a sneeze. And yet these scenes—
You reach for a book with a purple cover; you ask
If anyone has seen the sunset; the telephone rings
As the last guest bends into his overcoat—these things
That have and have not happened are central, if not to
The dark puzzle of your life, then at the heart of the world.

Pictures in a Gallery

1 TAPPY BEACH, "THE GATEWAY"

Two masonry columns
Perhaps six feet in height
Partly overgrown with
Some kind of dead rambler
Rose or suchlike, their tops
Surmounted by two bleak
Wooden discs, faded, cracked,
Inscribed with the place's
Name now illegibly
Gray: the left hand one is
Tilted—to judge from where
The writing used to be—
At an angle perhaps
Of twenty-five degrees.
Painted as if seen through
The open windows of
A passing car always
By a wondering child.

2 DICTYS CRETENSIS, "TOWERS OF FIRE"

. . . then they came into our city from out
Of the middle of it. They had waited.
I saw by firelight flashing off their brass,
By scintillations of their long spear points,
The burning that was going on even

Behind us, and I ran then through clanging
Passageways long and dark then out into
The galloping solitude of the sky
Which sped back past me as I, motionless,
Ran down to the ships. My wife and children
Were dead, my father was unbearable
And left in a corner of the cold floor.
Alone, my burdens were my companions.

3 JOHN PORTUGAL, "NIGHT SERIES, NO. 48"

There is nothing here but light
And dark and possibly one
Thing more: the question whether
The unspeakable divide
Between them on the canvas
Is indeed part of what is
Here, as much a part as the
Light, the dark, and the question.
We must learn to interpret
This, though, through a more central
Departure of light from out
Of the head of darkness where
It had remained as a kind
Of reminder: so the moon
Sets and leaves dark night with a
Valediction forbidding
Morning or the like, and which
The faithful darkness may try
To observe, for all we know,
Its failure being our light.

4 WALTER HUHN, "WAVES OF GRASS"

Ha ha, yes——one can almost see them move, the shining green
Crests, the plashings of light given back to light, the duller
Troughs of shadow moving broadly across the whole surface.
Yes. Very good. Except that the effect only works up
And down over the canvas hung there on the grey stone wall.
I remember deep ivy high on a grey stone wall blown
By cold winds on a sunny day in an unusual
June, sighing like a verdant sea; covering the old land
Of grey; engulfing the glassy lakes that shine up at me
Through a plane's window on bright flights, blindingly; embedding
The images that might peer out of such ponds (at the boys
Darting sudden looks into them from the brink—old towers
High on the bank behind them, tresses of nearby willows,
The gaily-poisoned darts of their own sudden faces fixed
For a moment's shaded eternity of charming gaze);
Whelming green floods over the mortared cracks between acres
Of field stone. It moved up and down the many-storeyed wall
As if across a realm of green I was looking down at.
Yes, yes. Very good. Except that there are no distances
In this picture and the green has put an end to no world
Save the barren plain of canvas, and the hopeful emptiness
With which it awaited its drowning. Come along, kiddo.

5 ANONYMOUS MASTER, "STANDING FIGURE"

A painting of a carved stone figure—
Why? Around the base can barely be
   Discerned the title of
   The piece: *Taking up Space* . . .

Of course, the painting, full of the rich
Light of contrivance, could hardly have
    That for a name; yet it
    Seems full of sympathy

For the sculptor working in darkness,
Being deprived of the light cast by
    Having to invent space,
    Telling flat lies about

What depth is, and where, which light depicts.
The literalness of shaping a
    Mass is like a kind of
    Groping around in a

Midnight of thick fact: no wonder that
Most of the time it all ends up as
    A nasty statuette,
    A blunt instrument, a

Dangerous spiky object in the
Corner, an equestrian figure
    Of *El Liberador,*
    Jefe del Guano, a

Statue to invite to lunch. Taking
Up space in both of one's hands, shaking
    It and thereby making
    A something out of it—

That would be different. That would mean
Marble clanging out in sweet pain, stone
    That had clung to all its
    Echoes until then;

That would mean a carved form that had been
Born of the same high struggle for depth
   As the noble distance
   Between two muddy smears

Of red, unloaded by the speaking
Brush, quickened by the spirit of breadth:
   Form sufficient to have
   Been drawn, yet free to stand.

6 J. KINNOR, "THE FINAL LUTE"

Hark, what discord: only one broken string
Is left, wiggling in a thin wormlike way
On the instrument's gray belly. The sky
Has had its bits of light picked out of it
And is itself hanging by a few strings
From what is behind it all. The last chord
Snapped into silence, echoing its sigh,
Long before the heavy light in this scene
Had composed itself, late light with the dark
In her arms. And, anecdotal pictures
Being what they are, that dark may be deemed
All there will be after what there is now
Has done with its unfolding. As for the
Painter's lights and darks themselves, there is no
Struggle among them even of embrace—
Even of the shadow of some final
Showdown that had been put off all this time.
If the flat shadow in the room behind
The silent instrument could speak, it would
Say *"My heart is a suspended struggle,*
Strike me, and it will crash noiselesssly to
An invisible floor in a strange land

Below what can been seen in the picture."
Shadow will join shadow, crowding, on an
Inaudible note of acquiescence,
The last aftermath of dark with concord.

At the End of the Day

The mere green of the conifers:
Against it the jubilantly
Dying leaves of late October
Cried out as against steadfastness;

The evening red in which we were
Dissolved was absorbed in itself
And hardly shone at all beyond
The dark windows of Finisterre;

Underfoot lay the mudded brown,
The color of the fallen thrush,
Of silence come, waiting to make
Dark of those wild hues and their cries.

Nox Regina

Why does she permit far
Too much to come to pass
Deep in her dominion,
Darkness to be so full
Of possibility:
So much making of love,
So much quiet dying
And, crowded with its paled
Allusions to the day
And all his regular
Brightness, so much dreaming?
These should be sorted out
And not allowed to lie
Against one another
Like, say, a scalpel, two
Mirrors, a painted bead,
And most of an old queen
Of spades in a dark drawer.
Why then does she not rule
Her lands more decently?
—Oh, she is lonely and
Her many eyes, dimly
Turned down on us as if
Glimmering, all are blind.

Notes

Blue Wine: I visited Saul Steinberg one afternoon and found that he had pasted some mock (or rather, visionary) wine labels on bottles, which were then filled with a substance I could not identify. This poem is an attempt to make sense out of what was apparently in them. In the mock-Homeric part of the poem, *Bhel* is named for the Indo-European base for "bright" or "shining," and *Kel* for one associated with "breaking." *Vin albastru* is blue wine in Rumanian.

Monuments: *that Face:* Medusa's

A Statue of Something: I had in mind William Rush's allegory of the Schuylkill, and the later of Thomas Eakins's paintings of Rush and his model; but the fable is independent of these.

The Train: *Sleepers* are another name for railroad crossties. *The Fair* was the New York World's Fair of 1939–40. Buttons saying *I Have Seen the Future* were distributed there.

Lyrical Interval: This was written in lieu of a song-cycle; it is as much about song-texts as it is a candidate for setting. The prologue and piano interlude are paraphrases of purely instrumental passages.

The Viewer: The dedicatee dreamed of seeing her own yellow bedroom (with, among other things, a copy of a Van Dyck self-portrait) through a mysterious optical viewer: this was written to demystify it. Britomart's mirror (*The Faerie Queene*, III, ii) showed a prophetic glimpse of her lover—I think *The Magic Flute* is more familiar.

Pictures in a Gallery: The titles are important, but the names of the artists are as private, and as unnecessary to the texts, as the titles of many abstract expressionist paintings.

Nox Regina: "Night, the Queen"—not *regina noctis*, who would be Mozart's Astrafiammante.

The Johns Hopkins University Press

*This book was composed in Linotype Baskerville text
and Bell italic display type by
Maryland Linotype Composition Company, Inc.,
from a design by Alan Carter. It was printed
and bound by the Maple Press Company.*

Library of Congress Cataloging in Publication Data

Hollander, John.
  Blue wine and other poems.

  (Johns Hopkins, poetry and fiction)
  I. Title. II. Series.
PS3515.03485B55   811'.5'4   78–20514
ISBN 0–8018–2209–2
ISBN 0–8018–2221–1 pbk.